Original title:
Echoes of Love

Copyright © 2024 Swan Charm
All rights reserved.

Author: Mirell Mesipuu
ISBN HARDBACK: 978-9916-89-217-6
ISBN PAPERBACK: 978-9916-89-218-3
ISBN EBOOK: 978-9916-89-219-0

Intertwined Loyalties

In whispers shared beneath the trees,
Two souls connect with gentle ease.
Bound by trust that weaves so tight,
Loyalty shines like stars at night.

Through trials faced and storms we brave,
Together strong, we rise, we save.
Each promise made, a thread we tie,
Forevermore, just you and I.

Faded Footprints in the Sand

Along the shore, our laughter played,
In golden sun, sweet memories laid.
Footprints linger, then fade away,
Time's tide comes in to softly sway.

Yet in my heart, they still remain,
The echoes of joy, love's sweet refrain.
Though the sands shift and rush to land,
I cherish each step, hand in hand.

Shadows that Embrace

Beneath the moon's soft silver glow,
Our shadows dance, a silent show.
In twilight calm, we find our peace,
Where worries fade and troubles cease.

The world may change, but here we stand,
Connected still, heart in hand.
In every shadow, love imparts,
Together woven, our tender hearts.

Summons of the Heart

In the stillness, a whisper calls,
The heart's desire, through silence falls.
With every beat, a song it sings,
Of hope and love and fragile wings.

Beyond the reach of time and space,
The soul responds to love's embrace.
In every glance, a spark ignites,
A summons deep, through endless nights.

The Current of Affection

In soft currents, whispers flow,
Beneath the trees, where love does grow.
Gentle touch upon the skin,
A dance of souls, where we begin.

In twilight's hue, our shadows blend,
A sacred bond, we will defend.
In laughter shared and silent tears,
We navigate through all our fears.

Like rivers winding, we entwine,
In every glance, your heart meets mine.
Through storms and sun, we pave our way,
Together strong, come what may.

When nights are long and dreams are bright,
We find our stars, our guiding light.
In every heartbeat, love's embrace,
In lasting moments, find our place.

Tapestry of Togetherness

Threads of fate, woven so tight,
In every day, we find our light.
Colors bright, in harmony,
A tapestry of you and me.

In laughter's sound, a song we weave,
In shared moments, hearts believe.
With every stitch, a story told,
In warmth and comfort, let love unfold.

Through seasons change, we stand as one,
In shadowed paths, we've just begun.
With threads of gold, and dreams in sight,
Together, we'll paint the night so bright.

In simple joys and heartfelt sighs,
We build our dreams under open skies.
A tapestry vast, beyond all measure,
In every moment, find our treasure.

Whispers of Affection

In quiet moments, whispers play,
Secrets shared at end of day.
Gentle breeze through tender leaves,
A dance of love, the heart believes.

With every glance, a spark ignites,
In shadows soft, our hearts take flight.
In silence, knowing, hands entwined,
In whispers soft, our souls aligned.

As night descends, the stars awake,
In sacred dreams, we softly break.
With whispered words, we find our way,
In love's embrace, forever stay.

Through quiet hours, spirits blend,
In every whisper, love's transcend.
In every heartbeat, echoes sweet,
In tender moments, our souls meet.

Reverberations of the Heart

In echoing chambers, feelings rise,
Soft reverberations 'neath the skies.
With every pulse, the rhythm speaks,
A dance of love, eternal peaks.

Through valleys deep and mountains high,
Our hearts compose a lullaby.
With gentle notes, we weave the sound,
In harmonies where love is found.

In quiet spaces, echoes swell,
Of whispered tales that hearts can tell.
In every moment, time stands still,
In resonance, we find our will.

As waves of passion crash and fall,
Through echoes vast, we heed the call.
In every heartbeat, strong and true,
The reverberation sings of you.

Canvas of Days Gone By

Faded hues and twilight skies,
Brushstrokes of forgotten sighs.
Memories linger, soft and bright,
Captured in the fading light.

A palette rich with tales untold,
Whispers of love, brave and bold.
Each color sings a hidden song,
In this canvas, we belong.

Time's embrace, it paints and weaves,
Threads of laughter, dreams, and leaves.
Seasons change, yet here they stay,
In the strokes of yesterday.

Moments frozen, shadows cast,
Echoes of a fleeting past.
In every line, a heartbeats trace,
A history time can't erase.

So let us gaze and let us feel,
The beauty in what's now surreal.
For in this art, our stories lie,
On the canvas of days gone by.

A Dance Through Time

Spinning softly, stars align,
Rhythms pulse, a secret sign.
Step by step, we sway and glide,
Through the ages, side by side.

Echoes of a waltz once known,
In every twirl, a journey grown.
Whirling past on destiny's floor,
In this dance, we long for more.

Moments flash like fireflies,
Fleeting glances, tender sighs.
In the music, hearts entwine,
Lost in time's soft, sweet design.

With every breath, we leap and soar,
Painting dreams forevermore.
In the rhythm, we are free,
Two souls dancing, you and me.

Let time drift, let shadows play,
As we dance the night away.
In this moment, we transcend,
A timeless dance that has no end.

Imprints of What Was

Footprints left on sandy shores,
Tales of magic, love, and wars.
Every step, a story laid,
In the echo of dusk's parade.

Time's gentle hand has brushed our skin,
Marking where our lives begin.
The whispers of forgotten dreams,
Trace our hearts like flowing streams.

Memories linger, soft and clear,
In the silence, we draw near.
Imprints etched on fabric rare,
Moments captured, laid bare.

Hints of laughter, shadows cast,
Linking futures with the past.
In every crease and faded line,
A tapestry of love divine.

As we walk through life's embrace,
We leave behind a sacred space.
In these traces, we shall find,
What was lost, and intertwined.

Timeless Murmurs

In the hush of twilight's breath,
Murmurs linger, life and death.
Voices of the past still sigh,
In the stillness, time slips by.

Timeless tales in shadows weave,
Secrets held by those who believe.
In the breeze, we hear their call,
Whispers of the ancients fall.

Through the echoes, we may roam,
Finding joy in what feels home.
Each soft murmur, a guiding light,
Illuminating the darkest night.

From the depths of ages old,
Stories rise, enchantments told.
In the quiet, we connect,
Timeless whispers we respect.

So let us listen, hearts awake,
To the murmurs that time can make.
In every whisper, we'll derive,
The timeless truths that keep us alive.

Notes from the Depths

In shadows where whispers dwell,
Secrets in silence swell.
Echoes of memories call,
Beneath the waves, we fall.

Ink spills on paper deep,
Stories of dreams we keep.
Drifting in currents slow,
Writing what we cannot show.

Lost treasures of the heart,
In oceans, we're torn apart.
Searching for what was once,
In the depths, we take a plunge.

Voices that softly sing,
Carried by the tide's swing.
Beneath the stars so bright,
Notes of longing in the night.

Finding peace in the dark,
Illuminated by a spark.
In the void, we find a way,
Notes from the depths, here to stay.

Pulses of Connection

Hearts beat in perfect time,
Rhythms that flow like rhyme.
In every glance we share,
A bond beyond compare.

Threads woven deep and tight,
In the day and through the night.
Silent words all around,
In this love, we are found.

Whispers that travel far,
Guided by a shooting star.
Through the storms, through the calm,
Our union is a balm.

Electric in the air,
Feelings we can only share.
Together we ignite,
Pulses of connection, light.

Forever intertwined,
In the fabric, love aligned.
A symphony we create,
In every heartbeat, fate.

Gentle Ripples of Desire

Softly the waters sigh,
As the moon drifts in the sky.
Whispers of wishes flow,
In the night, desires grow.

Fingers trace the cool sand,
Yearning for a warm hand.
Moments that linger sweet,
In the dance of hearts, we meet.

Breathless under the stars,
Hopes echo from afar.
Each glance a gentle tease,
Carried in the evening breeze.

Waves crash, then pull away,
Leaving traces of the day.
In the twilight's embrace,
Ripples in this sacred space.

With every surge and swell,
In the silence, we can tell.
The longing's quiet plight,
Gentle ripples speak of night.

Lost Lyrics of Us

Once we sang a sweet song,
Harmony where we belonged.
Now the notes fade away,
In the silence, we decay.

In whispers of the past,
Moments we thought would last.
But shadows keep us bound,
In echoes, we're lost and drowned.

Pages turn with each sigh,
Lyrics that never die.
But chapters drift apart,
Leaving spaces in the heart.

Melodies now unplayed,
In the twilight, we've strayed.
Harmonies left behind,
Lost lyrics, undefined.

In every fading tone,
Our stories can be known.
If we listen deeply still,
Perhaps a song, we will.

Lullabies of Memory

In the stillness of the night,
Whispers of dreams take flight.
Soft reflections gently sway,
Carrying moments lost in play.

Through the corridors of my mind,
Echoes of laughter intertwined.
Familiar faces float like clouds,
In the silence, they call aloud.

Time weaves a tapestry so bright,
Colors of joy, shadows of light.
Each stitch holds a tender tale,
Of love that will never pale.

Every heartbeat sings a song,
Guiding where we both belong.
In the corners where we reside,
Lullabies of memory never hide.

As dawn breaks, the past awakes,
Fleeting glances, tender stakes.
In the warmth of morning's hue,
Memories dance, forever new.

Faded Notes of Tenderness

In an old box, notes remain,
Faded scripts of joy and pain.
Each word a whisper from the past,
Moments cherished, meant to last.

A gentle touch, a soft embrace,
Carried echoes of your grace.
Love's sweet melody plays on repeat,
In the heart, its rhythm beats.

Through the pages, shadows weave,
Promises made and dreams to cleave.
In the silence, love finds a way,
Guiding us through night and day.

The ink may fade, but feelings hold,
Stories of warmth like threads of gold.
In every note, a piece of you,
Faded yet bright, forever true.

As twilight falls, the music sighs,
Each lost note a soft goodbye.
Yet in my heart, they ever dwell,
Faded notes of tenderness tell.

Chimes of the Soul

Beneath the stars, the silence sings,
Chimes of joy, the night winds bring.
Each note dances like a breeze,
A symphony among the trees.

In the stillness, hearts unite,
Resonating in pure delight.
Every echo tells a tale,
Of dreams that dare to set sail.

The moonlight casts a silver glow,
Illuminating paths we know.
With each chime, a story unfold,
Whispers of warmth, tales retold.

Through the ages, melodies flow,
Guiding us, where we go.
In every note, the soul connects,
Chimes of love, what life respects.

As dawn's first light begins to break,
The harmony of hearts awake.
In every sunrise, we find our role,
Embracing life, chimes of the soul.

Ghosts of Sweet Embrace

In corners where shadows play,
Ghosts of sweet embrace stay.
Memories linger, softly spun,
In the warmth of setting sun.

Flickering lights in empty rooms,
Whispers echo, love still blooms.
Each sigh a breath of times gone past,
In our hearts, these moments last.

Though the fabric of time may fray,
These spirits guide us everyday.
In tender glances, we still find,
The essence of love intertwined.

Through the whispers of the night,
They remind us of pure light.
In the softness of their grace,
We feel the warmth of their embrace.

As we journey, hand in hand,
Ghosts of love, they understand.
In sweet remembrance, we dance free,
Holding on to our history.

Pulse of an Unseen Bond

In whispers shared, our hearts align,
Invisible threads, a sacred sign.
Through time and distance, love persists,
A gentle force that can't be missed.

Moments captured, an eternal glow,
In laughter's echo, you always know.
As shadows dance beneath the moon,
Our souls entwined, a soft, sweet tune.

Through storms we weather, hand in hand,
A silent promise, forever planned.
In every heartbeat, we're intertwined,
A pulse of love that knows no bind.

Each glance exchanged, a story told,
In secret glances, our truth unfolds.
The universe whispers, and we listen,
To the bond unseen, our hearts glisten.

In every silence, we find our peace,
A quiet joy that will never cease.
Together we flow like rivers wide,
In this unseen bond, forever side by side.

The Chime of Lost Tomorrows

In twilight's glow, dreams softly fade,
Echoes linger in the light's cascade.
The chime of moments that slipped away,
Whispers of paths we chose not to stay.

Once vibrant hopes, now shadows cast,
We chase the specters of the past.
With every tick, the clock reminds,
Of futures lost and time that blinds.

Yet in the silence, a song remains,
Of laughter, love, and sweet refrains.
The chime resounds, a haunting call,
Inviting us to rise, never fall.

Through winding roads, we find our way,
Each step a treasure, come what may.
In the echo's heart, we learn to grow,
From the chimes of lost tomorrows below.

In every heartbeat, there lies a chance,
A melody sweet, a timeless dance.
Though tomorrows may shift and bend,
The chime of memories shall never end.

In the Realm of Remembrance

In twilight's grasp, the past awakes,
Through dreams we wander, the heart quakes.
In gentle hues, the memories call,
A tapestry woven, encompassing all.

Faces and laughter, in shadows play,
Each moment, a treasure that won't decay.
In nostalgia's embrace, we find our way,
The realm of remembrance, where hearts sway.

Stories linger in the dusky air,
Whispers of love beyond compare.
With every glance, a time retraced,
In the warm glow, none are replaced.

Moments shared beneath starlit skies,
In silence, we hear the softest sighs.
Time may march, but love's refrain,
In this realm of remembrance, will ever remain.

Through the corridors of our hearts we roam,
In the realm of remembrance, we find our home.
With every heartbeat, the past holds tight,
In love's embrace, we find our light.

Trails of Tenderness

In gentle whispers, kindness flows,
A path of love, where warmth bestows.
With every step, a story we weave,
In trails of tenderness, we believe.

Through stormy nights and sunlit days,
Compassion guides in countless ways.
In fleeting moments, hearts ignite,
Creating memories that shine so bright.

With open arms, we bear the load,
In the softness of touch, a love bestowed.
Through shared laughter and gentle tears,
We walk together, facing our fears.

In every heartbeat, a promise made,
In trails of tenderness, our souls parade.
With every glance, understanding grows,
In the warmth of love, the heart knows.

As seasons change and time may bend,
In trails of tenderness, we ascend.
So let us wander, hand in hand,
In the circle of love, forever we stand.

The Pulse of Shared Journeys

Two souls tread paths anew,
With every step, they grow.
Unspoken ties weave strong,
Guiding them as they flow.

In laughter, they find light,
In shadows, they take flight.
Moments shared in twilight,
A bond that feels just right.

Through valleys low and high,
They chase the painted sky.
Each heartbeat, a soft sigh,
A journey, sweet and spry.

Hurdles met with bold grace,
Together, they embrace.
With dreams they interlace,
Life unfolds, no haste.

And as the stars align,
Their spirits intertwine.
In every pulse, they find
The beauty of time's design.

A Chorus of Shared Solitude

In silence, hearts can sing,
Whispers of the unseen.
Two souls share the same ground,
In stillness, love's serene.

Lonely streets echo soft,
Footsteps rise and drift aloft.
In each pause, a warmth grows,
A bond that lights from soft.

The world may spin apart,
Yet here, they form a chart.
With quiet, tender grace,
They map the lines of heart.

Through windows, light breaks in,
Illuminating kin.
They find strength in the hush,
Counting stars, no rush.

In solitude's embrace,
They find a sacred space.
In echoes of their dreams,
A chorus softly seems.

Lingering Lullabies

Soft whispers float on air,
A melody so rare.
In twilight's gentle sigh,
Dreams drift without a care.

Crickets hum a sweet tune,
Beneath the watchful moon.
Each note, a tender grace,
In harmony, they croon.

Their voices blend as one,
A symphony begun.
Lullabies to the stars,
Till day has come undone.

With every stroke of night,
They weave a story bright.
In laughter, in soft cries,
They chase the fading light.

As dawn begins to rise,
They close their sleepy eyes.
In dreams, they'll find the song,
That lingers in the skies.

Holding onto the Echoes

In shadows, memories bloom,
Whispers fill the room.
With every step they trace,
Past loves begin to loom.

Faint laughter drifts like leaves,
Wrapped in the heart's sleeves.
Each moment, a soft ghost,
In silence, heaves and weaves.

They gather echoes near,
In twilight's lingering sphere.
With every spoken word,
The past, they hold it dear.

Through corridors of time,
They search for a sweet rhyme.
In every breath, a sigh,
They find their hearts in chime.

And as the day does fade,
In memories, they wade.
Holding onto echoes bright,
In love's soft serenade.

The Sound of Togetherness

In the quiet we find our peace,
Voices blend, worries cease.
Harmony wraps us in its fold,
A story shared, a bond so bold.

Laughter dances in the air,
Every moment, we truly care.
Hand in hand, we face the day,
Together, come what may.

The stars above, they shine as one,
Guiding us till the day is done.
In the melody of our hearts,
Together is where the joy starts.

Through trials, our spirits connect,
In every smile, we reflect.
Building dreams on this sweet ground,
In each other, solace found.

The sound of laughter, a gentle song,
In this unity, we belong.
With every note, our love expands,
In the embrace of joined hands.

Shadows of Desire

In the twilight, whispers grow,
Longing dances, soft and slow.
Hidden dreams begin to gleam,
Caught within a midnight dream.

Eyes that linger, hearts that race,
Each glance a secret, every pace.
In the shadows, passions play,
Drawing closer, come what may.

Silken threads entwined with fate,
In the silence, we await.
Every heartbeat, every sigh,
Beneath the stars, we fly high.

Words unspoken, yet so clear,
In the dark, we feel no fear.
Desires bloom in moonlit grace,
Finding solace in embrace.

The night is ours, a sacred space,
In shadows deep, we find our place.
Together lost, forever bound,
In this world, our love profound.

Harmonies of Longing

Echoes of a distant tune,
Whisper secrets to the moon.
Every note, a wish untold,
Harmonies of dreams unfold.

In the silence, hear the call,
Longing for what feels like all.
Fingers tracing every sound,
In this rhythm, lost, we're found.

Every heartbeat syncs as one,
Melodies where we have begun.
In the dusk, our spirits blend,
Chasing wishes that never end.

Through the verses of the night,
Searching always for the light.
Every hum, a gentle plea,
In the music, you and me.

As our souls begin to soar,
In the echoes, we explore.
In longing's arms, we softly sway,
Together, come what may.

Songs from the Past

Memories wrapped in faded sound,
In the echoes, love is found.
A sweet refrain from days of yore,
In every note, we long for more.

Footsteps dance on ancient ground,
In the silence, joy's profound.
Every moment, a cherished rhyme,
In this song, we pause for time.

Sunset colors the skies so bright,
Shadows fade into the night.
As we sing our timeless tune,
Visions glide beneath the moon.

Heartfelt verses, stories spun,
Through the laughter, we are one.
In the ballads, dreams take flight,
Carried forth on waves of light.

Songs from the past, forever clear,
In our hearts, they linger near.
In their warmth, we find our way,
Guided by the love we play.

Glimmers of Forgotten Affections

In shadows where memories dance,
Whispers of love, a fleeting chance.
Faded echoes of sweet refrain,
Lost in the heart, yet never in vain.

Glimmers bright, in twilight's haze,
Unraveled threads of simpler days.
A soft touch, a knowing glance,
In the silence, a hopeful chance.

Time may dim the brightest flame,
Yet in the soul, we find the same.
A flicker ignites, a spark so rare,
Breath of nostalgia fills the air.

Each heartbeat speaks of what was lost,
But warmth remains despite the cost.
In every sigh, the past still gleams,
Heart flows gently with ancient dreams.

Through tempest winds and shifting skies,
The fire within never truly dies.
In the quiet, a promise clings,
Life renews as the memory sings.

Heartbeats in the Quiet

Amidst the chaos, a gentle pulse,
Echoes of love, where time convulse.
In stillness found, two souls entwined,
A heartbeat whispers, softly aligned.

Night wraps around like velvet deep,
Secrets shared, in silence we keep.
The world may fade, but here we stand,
Heartbeats rhythm, hand in hand.

Each moment lingers, soft and sweet,
In every silence, our spirits meet.
A glance exchanged, a breath held tight,
In heart's embrace, we find our light.

Days may pass like clouds on high,
Yet in the quiet, we still fly.
In written stars, our dreams ignite,
Through every shadow, we find the bright.

Listen closely, feel the grace,
In the quiet, we find our place.
A symphony of hearts in tune,
Forever playing, night to noon.

Whispered Secrets Beneath the Moon

Below the moon's silver glow,
Whispers travel, soft and low.
Secrets shared in hushed delight,
Promises woven through the night.

Stars bear witness, silent and bright,
Fates entwined in sacred flight.
Each word dances on gentle air,
Bound by trust, a sacred prayer.

In shadows deep, our hearts explore,
Every glance opens a door.
Soft touches linger, secrets bloom,
In the quiet, love finds room.

Night's embrace wraps us tight,
In whispered tones, we take our flight.
The world fades, just us two,
Beneath the moon, dreams come true.

Together we spin tales untold,
In the dark, our ffutures unfold.
With every sigh, a bond transcends,
In whispered nights, the journey bends.

The Canvas of Us

With strokes of fate, we painted skies,
Colors blending, where passion lies.
A canvas vast, our spirits soar,
Each hue a memory, forevermore.

In the light of day, bold and bright,
In the dark, soft as starlight.
Brushes dance in rhythm and flow,
Creating tales only we know.

Every sigh a stroke anew,
In shades of love, in deepest blue.
Together we craft, with careful touch,
Art of the heart that means so much.

The canvas shifts with every breath,
Bold in life, defying death.
In every line, a story told,
In strokes of life, our hearts unfold.

So let us paint with joy and grace,
The masterpiece of our embrace.
In every moment, vibrant and true,
The canvas holds the essence of us two.

Threads of Affection

Woven gently, soft and light,
In your laughter, I find delight.
Every glance, a silent thread,
Binding hearts where love has led.

Moments shared, we stitch each day,
In our hearts, they softly lay.
Tangled dreams beneath the stars,
In their glow, we've traveled far.

Through the storms and sunny skies,
Together, we shall always rise.
With each heartbeat, love's design,
Forever yours, and you are mine.

Fingers laced in whispered sighs,
Every promise softly ties.
In this dance, we weave our fate,
A tapestry, love isn't late.

Threads that shine through joy and pain,
In every loss, in every gain.
Through the years, they intertwine,
Eternal love, our hearts align.

Sighs in the Twilight

As the sun dips low and fades,
Soft whispers in the evening glades.
Shadows stretch and softly creep,
In twilight's grasp, the world does sleep.

The stars emerge, a silver hue,
In this moment, I think of you.
A gentle breeze, a secret sigh,
Beneath the canvas of the sky.

Memories surface, bright and clear,
In quiet solitude, you're near.
The twilight speaks of days gone by,
In each breath, a longing sigh.

Colors blend, night takes its throne,
In every heartbeat, I am known.
Wrapped in dusk, our dreams ignite,
Together we drift into the night.

Eclipsed by shadows, love still glows,
In the silence, our passion flows.
Through sighs and whispers, I do find,
In twilight's arms, you're intertwined.

Lingering Hues of Heartache

Faded photos, whispers low,
In echoes of love, memories flow.
Crimson leaves on autumn's breath,
Beauty lingers even in death.

Every moment, a soft regret,
In shadows cast, our hearts beset.
With every dawn, the pain anew,
Lingering hues of me and you.

Through the silence, I search in vain,
For the solace hidden in pain.
Yet in the ache, I find a spark,
Illuminating love's last mark.

Waves of sorrow crash on the shore,
I gather strength to feel once more.
From ashes, colors start to bloom,
In heartache's dark, there's still room.

With remnants of a love once bright,
I stitch the wounds, restore the light.
Through every scar, a story glows,
In lingering hues, my heart still knows.

Harmonics of Hope

In a world where shadows dwell,
Hope resounds like a gentle bell.
With every note, a dream takes flight,
Harmonies dance in the soft moonlight.

Through the storms and darkest days,
A melody in countless ways.
In every heartbeat, faith will rise,
A song of truth beneath the skies.

With open arms, tomorrow calls,
In its embrace, my spirit thralls.
Each whisper sings of paths to roam,
In the symphony, we find our home.

Resilience flows in every chord,
In the struggle, love's reward.
From echoes past, a future bright,
In harmonics, we take flight.

Together, we'll write our refrain,
In every joy, in every pain.
Hope unites, it's our decree,
In this chorus, we are free.

Vibrations of a Shared Heart

In the stillness, whispers flow,
Echoes of a love we both know.
Heartbeat dances, soft and sweet,
In this rhythm, two souls meet.

Fingers intertwined, time stands still,
Every glance ignites, a thrill.
In our silence, languages blend,
A melody that will never end.

Stars above watch our embrace,
In this moment, we find our place.
Vibrations pull us, side by side,
In the harmony, we confide.

Through the shadows, light will spark,
Tracing paths etched in the dark.
With every heartbeat, love ignites,
Vibrations echo through the nights.

Underneath the moon's soft rays,
We'll dance through life's winding maze.
As two notes create a song,
In this love, we both belong.

Serenade of Silent Promises

A quiet night, the stars aligned,
Silhouettes of dreams combined.
Promises linger in the air,
With every breath, we share a dare.

Soft whispers in the gentle breeze,
A serenade that puts hearts at ease.
In the shadows, secrets spill,
Silent vows that time can't kill.

Eyes like oceans, deep and bright,
In this symphony, we unite.
No words needed for this tune,
Underneath the silver moon.

Like petals falling, love unfolds,
In silent stories, our future holds.
Every heartbeat a promise made,
A serenade that won't soon fade.

Together we journey, hand in hand,
Through the silence, we'll make our stand.
In the quiet, love will rise,
A melody that never dies.

The Symphony We Created

In the orchestra of twilight, we play,
Each note a memory, night and day.
Strings of laughter, drums of tears,
In this symphony, we face our fears.

Every glance a chord, sweetly struck,
In the rhythm of love, we find our luck.
A crescendo builds with every sigh,
As we dance beneath the endless sky.

With every heartbeat, a new refrain,
Melodies linger, like soft rain.
In harmony, our futures blend,
A symphony that will never end.

Together we write this timeless score,
Each measure echoing forevermore.
In the silence, we find our beat,
In this orchestra, love is complete.

As the final note begins to fade,
We'll carry this tune, unafraid.
For in each moment, a song we've spun,
The symphony rises, two become one.

Chords of Intimacy

In the quiet, secrets live,
Every laugh, the heart will give.
Chords of intimacy softly play,
Binding souls in a gentle sway.

Whispers shared under the stars,
Transformed silence, healing scars.
In this bond, our fingers trace,
A melody that time can't erase.

Through the trials, we find our song,
Every note marks where we belong.
In the space between, love unfolds,
Chords of warmth that never get old.

With every chapter, we compose,
A symphony that always grows.
In this dance of tender grace,
Chords of intimacy embrace.

As twilight deepens, hearts ignite,
In this rhythm, we find our light.
Together we'll sing, come what may,
Chords of intimacy lead the way.

The Light We Shared

In twilight's gentle arms we stand,
Each whisper soft, a fleeting brand.
As shadows dance, the stars ignite,
Reminding us of shared delight.

The laughter lingers in the air,
A melody that soothes our care.
Through memories bright, we find our way,
In every moment, come what may.

Though years may pass, and paths may part,
The light we shared stays in the heart.
Together forged, in every tear,
A bond that time will not endear.

With every sunrise, dreams unfold,
A story told in threads of gold.
In echoes soft, our spirits blend,
For love's embrace knows no true end.

As shadows fall, we chase the dawn,
In silent vows, forever drawn.
Through every storm, we'll stand the test,
The light we shared, our timeless quest.

Letters from Another Time

In faded ink, the words reside,
A whispered past where dreams abide.
With every page, a tale unfolds,
Of loves once lost and secrets told.

From distant shores, they call our names,
In echoes soft, like flickering flames.
With every line, the heart remembers,
A dance of souls through cold Novembers.

These letters bear the weight of time,
In fragile hope, a tender rhyme.
They bridge the gaps, they mend the tears,
A testament to all our years.

Through ink and paper, laughter soars,
A glimpse of life behind closed doors.
In every heartbeat, dreams entwined,
A symphony of love defined.

So let me read the words anew,
Each letter holding thoughts of you.
In timeless depth and echoes sweet,
A past revived, in memories meet.

In the Space Between

Between the silence of our sighs,
A universe of whispered ties.
In shadows cast, our shadows blend,
A hidden world that will not end.

In every glance, a story stirs,
A language spoken without words.
Through heartbeats lost, we drift and sway,
In the space where dreams hold sway.

These fleeting moments, soft and light,
As day embraces the coming night.
Invisible threads pull us near,
In softest whispers, sweet and clear.

Our souls unite as time stands still,
In perfect harmony, we feel.
The world outside fades from view,
In the space between, it's just us two.

So close your eyes, let spirit roam,
Through realms of love, we find our home.
In dreams that weave with gentle grace,
Forget the world, just find your place.

Harmonized Reveries

In twilight's glow, the music plays,
A symphony of golden rays.
Each note a breath, a gentle sigh,
In harmonies, our spirits fly.

With every chord, the heart responds,
In rhythmic dance, the night absconds.
The melodies of memories wake,
In every heartbeat, dreams partake.

We drift on clouds of softest sound,
In sacred rhythm, love is found.
As starlit notes descend like rain,
We savor joy, we kiss the pain.

Through every whisper, hopes ignite,
In harmonized, enchanting light.
Together lost in sweet refrain,
A symphony that knows no chain.

Let music guide our wandering souls,
In every echo, love consoles.
For in this realm of notes and dreams,
Our hearts unite, or so it seems.

Reverie Through Time

In quiet moments, shadows play,
A whisper of dreams from yesterday.
Through corridors of time we roam,
Chasing the echoes of a forgotten home.

Each heartbeat is a gentle call,
In stillness, we rise, in silence we fall.
Memories flicker, like stars on the rise,
Guiding us forward, beneath endless skies.

Reflections dance on the surface of thought,
Tales of our youth, each lesson we've sought.
Threads of our past, woven with care,
Bind us together, though life may seem rare.

Through the windows of time, we gaze in delight,
Chasing the shadows, embracing the light.
Each moment a treasure, each second a gift,
In the reverie of time, our spirits will lift.

So here we stand, hand in hand we bind,
A journey of heart, forever entwined.
In reverie through time, we find our way,
Amongst the whispers of yesterday's sway.

Underneath the Stars We Shared

Beneath the canvas of night's embrace,
We spoke of dreams, and time's endless chase.
Stars like diamonds twinkling bright,
A tapestry woven, our futures in sight.

Your laughter echoed in the cool, crisp air,
A moment of magic, a moment to share.
With every heartbeat, we dared to believe,
That love like this, we'd never deceive.

The moon cast shadows, a gentle glow,
In that fleeting moment, we let our hearts flow.
Whispers of promises, tender and true,
Underneath the stars, it was me and you.

Memories linger like the warmth of a song,
In the rhythmic pulse where we both belong.
Under the heavens, our spirits entwined,
A world full of wonder, so beautifully blind.

Though time may pass, and seasons may change,
The stars above us will never feel strange.
For underneath the stars, we forever will care,
In the silence of night, our dreams are laid bare.

A Dance of Lost Words

In the dim light, shadows gleam,
Words forgotten, lost in a dream.
Dancing softly on the edge of night,
Each syllable fading, yet burning bright.

Whispers linger like a ghostly sigh,
Echoes of love that once reached the sky.
A waltz of silence, where stories reside,
In the empty spaces, our souls collide.

Through tangled phrases and unspoken truths,
We learn the language of forgotten youths.
In every heartbeat, a story remains,
A dance with shadows, beneath the pains.

The rhythm of time, it sways and it bends,
In the dance of lost words, our journey transcends.
Each gesture a promise, pure and sincere,
That through the silence, love will persevere.

So let us move through this ethereal frame,
A dance of lost words, igniting the flame.
In the quietest corners, the heart finds its way,
In the echoes of absence, together we sway.

The Weaving of Yesterdays

Threads of memory, spun with care,
A tapestry rich, woven inair.
Each moment a stitch, each laugh a hue,
In the fabric of time, it's me and you.

In the loom of life, our stories entwine,
The colors of joy, the shades of the divine.
With whispers of heartbeats, we craft the design,
A masterpiece forming, a love so benign.

The echoes of laughter, the scent of the rain,
Each thread we create holds joy and holds pain.
In the weaving of yesterdays, we find our truth,
A narrative rich in the innocence of youth.

As seasons do change, and moments may fade,
The weaving continues, with memories laid.
In every encounter, in tears and in cheer,
Our story continues, forever sincere.

So let us embrace the fabric we've spun,
In the tapestry of life, we are never done.
With love as the warp, and trust as the weft,
In the weaving of yesterdays, we find our depth.

Whispers of the Heart

In shadows soft, secrets lie,
Where dreams and hopes quietly sigh.
A gentle touch, a fleeting glance,
The heart speaks loud in silent dance.

Longing echoes in the night,
Bathed in the soft, silver light.
Words unspoken, feelings shared,
In whispered truths, souls are bared.

Through tangled thoughts, we find our way,
Each heartbeat sings, come what may.
In every pause, a world unfolds,
Our stories whispered, yet so bold.

With every tear, a tale of grace,
Love finds refuge in time and space.
Like morning dew on waking grass,
These whispers bloom, forever last.

As stars ignite and darkness falls,
The heart's soft cadence gently calls.
In every whisper, love shall grow,
A timeless joy, forever flow.

Reflections in Time

Time dances slow on moments lost,
In every tick, we feel the cost.
Reflections cast on waters deep,
Memories linger, dreams to keep.

Past and present intertwine,
In the silence, shadows shine.
Each glance reveals a story spun,
Threads of laughter, tales begun.

Between the lines of faded notes,
The heart remembers, deeply gloats.
Puzzles pieced from days gone by,
In quiet whispers, we hear the sigh.

Time wraps love in soft embrace,
Every heartbeat finds its place.
In echoes' arms, we learn to see,
The beauty in life's tapestry.

As twilight wanes, we stand as one,
Reflecting on what has been done.
With every glance, histories bloom,
In the light, there's room for room.

Resonance of Affection

In every laugh, a sweet refrain,
Love's resonance, a soft chain.
Fingers entwined, hearts align,
In silence speaks a love divine.

Beneath the stars, we softly sway,
Our souls entangled, night and day.
In gentle whispers, secrets weave,
A tapestry of love we believe.

Each heartbeat echoes in the dark,
With every kiss, we leave a mark.
Resonant chords of joy and pain,
In harmony, we dance again.

Through trials faced and battles won,
Together, brighter than the sun.
In every glance, a promise lies,
Resonance of love never dies.

As seasons change and time moves fast,
In every moment, we are cast.
Anchored deep, our hearts fulfill,
In love's embrace, we always will.

Murmurs Beneath the Stars

Underneath the vast night sky,
Murmurs echo, dreams float high.
In the hush, where secrets swell,
Whispers weave a timeless spell.

Stars above, they blink and sway,
Guiding hearts that lose their way.
In gentle sighs, the world aligns,
With every murmur, love refines.

The moon conspires with the night,
Bathing us in silver light.
A tapestry of hopes anew,
In softest murmur, love shines through.

With every breath, the cosmos hums,
Emerging songs of what love becomes.
With whispered words, we find our peace,
In this stillness, our hearts release.

As dawn approaches, hints of gold,
The murmurs linger, tales unfold.
Beneath the stars, our souls ignite,
In tender whispers, love takes flight.

Fragments of a Love Story

In shadows of time, we whispered dreams,
Chasing reflections, or so it seems.
With every heartbeat, the echo grew,
A tapestry woven of me and you.

Fleeting glances beneath the moon,
Silent laughter, a soft tune.
Memories linger, like stars on a night,
Carried away in the dawn's gentle light.

Pages of letters, forgotten and torn,
Ink of emotions, the heart's early dawn.
Scattered pieces, we search the past,
Yet in the fragments, true love will last.

The warmth of your hand, a lingering touch,
In the silence, I've missed you so much.
Together we danced, a beautiful trance,
Holding our breath for a long-lost chance.

Even the silence has words unsaid,
In the garden of hopes, where heartbeats bled.
Each fragment a promise, written in fate,
Entwined forever, though time can't wait.

Threads of Yesteryear

Woven in time, each thread does connect,
Stories of moments we've come to respect.
The laughter, the tears, like ribbons they flow,
Stitched in our souls, creating a glow.

Faded photographs fill up the walls,
Echoes of laughter in nostalgic halls.
Each glance through the years, a tale to relive,
In the quilt of our lives, so much to forgive.

The fabric of dreams held tight in our hearts,
Every experience intricately imparts.
With the passage of time, we gather and spin,
Threads of yesteryear, where we've always been.

Like a gentle breeze, whispers remain,
In the silence, we still feel the pain.
Yet woven in hope, the future is bright,
Knots of our past, tied together in light.

In the loom of existence, we thread and we weave,
Crafting the tales that we dare to believe.
Each loss, every triumph, a stitch in our seams,
Threads of yesteryear, holding our dreams.

Fluid Moments of Passion

In a blink of an eye, the world fades away,
Where time seems to stop, in the light of the day.
With whispers of longing, the flames start to glow,
Caught in the dance, where only we know.

The scent of your skin, intoxicating and sweet,
A heartbeat in rhythm, our bodies compete.
In the fluid moments, undoubted and free,
With every glance shared, just you and me.

The touch of your fingers, a brush on my soul,
A surge of electric, igniting the whole.
Lost in the passion, the heat and the fire,
In these fleeting seconds, we rise even higher.

Every sigh carried on the breath of the night,
Illuminated by stars, our spirits take flight.
A canvas of feeling, we paint shades anew,
In these fluid moments, it's only us two.

As dawn starts to break, we linger and sigh,
Even as daylight is creeping nearby.
In the tapestry woven, our memories shine,
Fluid moments of passion, forever entwined.

The Pulse of Remembrance

In the quiet of night, your voice resonates,
A pulse of remembrance, never abates.
With shadows like whispers, the past starts to play,
In echoes of love, we find our way.

Time stretches and bends, like light through the glass,
Moments that shimmer, yet hours that pass.
We gather the fragments of light and of sound,
In the pulse of remembrance, love will surround.

Faded reflections dance under the stars,
Each heartbeat a rhythm, healing our scars.
We travel through memories, alive in the dream,
Finding the threads, unraveling the seam.

The past and the present entwined in a song,
As time marches forward, we still feel strong.
With every recollection, the heart finds its place,
The pulse of remembrance wraps us in grace.

So here we will stand, in the glow of the night,
With memories cherished, ablaze in the light.
In the heartbeat of moments, love never parts,
The pulse of remembrance forever imparts.

Resounding Romance

In twilight's glow, our whispers blend,
A symphony where hearts ascend.
Each glance a promise, softly made,
In love's embrace, we're unafraid.

Through moonlit walks, we gently sway,
With every breath, we find our way.
In laughter's echo, joy takes flight,
Together, hearts ignite the night.

With every star, our dreams align,
A timeless bond, your hand in mine.
As seasons change, our love remains,
In every joy, in every pain.

We carve our names in sands of time,
A dance of fate, a rhythmic rhyme.
In silent vows, our souls entwine,
Forevermore, your heart is mine.

As sunsets paint the sky in fire,
We weave our tale, a deep desire.
With each heartbeat, we grow anew,
In every moment, I choose you.

Fragments of Forever

A snapshot glance, a fleeting touch,
In sweet remembrance, we cling so much.
With every moment, life unfolds,
In scattered pieces, love beholds.

The laughter shared, a fleeting breeze,
In tiny fragments, we find our ease.
Through shadowed paths, we wander free,
In every heartbeat, you're part of me.

We gather dust from long-lost dreams,
In honest words, our truth redeems.
Each memory, a glimmer bright,
Reflects the warmth of love's pure light.

Like grains of sand, we slip away,
Yet in our hearts, we chose to stay.
In every sorrow, every cheer,
We find the fragments ever near.

The past embraced, the future calls,
In every rise, in every fall.
With open arms, we face the sun,
These fragments shine, two hearts as one.

Heartstrings in Harmony

In gentle chords, our melodies play,
As heartstrings hum in sweet array.
With each caress, a note is struck,
In perfect harmony, we find our luck.

Like birds in flight, we soar so high,
In sync we rise, to touch the sky.
Through whispered secrets, rhythms flow,
In every glance, our passions grow.

Together, we compose a song,
In love's embrace, where we belong.
With laughter bright, our spirits lift,
As heartstrings dance, a timeless gift.

In twilight's haze, the music swells,
With every touch, our story tells.
In symphony, our spirits fuse,
Together, we shall never lose.

Through life's duets, we gently sway,
In every note, we find our way.
With hands entwined, we brave the storm,
In heartstrings' grip, our hearts stay warm.

Reflections on a Tender Tomorrow

In dawn's soft light, our dreams awake,
Each quiet promise, love's sweet stake.
With every step, the day unfolds,
In tender whispers, our future's told.

We weave our hopes in golden thread,
With gentle hearts, toward love we're led.
As seasons turn, we stand as one,
In brighter tomorrows, we'll be spun.

With every smile, we build a bridge,
Across the waters, we freely ridge.
In shared laughter, life finds its grace,
In every moment, I see your face.

Through quiet nights, we dream anew,
With starry skies, our wishes brew.
In every heartbeat, a step we take,
Together forging, a path we make.

In tender tomorrows, hand in hand,
With love's embrace, we bravely stand.
For in our hearts, the best is yet,
In every memory, no regret.

Murmurs of the Beloved

In whispers soft, the night unfolds,
Secrets shared, among the cold.
Your breath a song, my heart's delight,
Beneath the stars, we claim the night.

With every glance, a story spun,
Two souls entwined, forever one.
In gentle hugs, the world retreats,
Your love, my solace, my heart beats.

Through shadows cast, and dreams anew,
In quiet moments, I find you.
Your laughter dances on the breeze,
A melody that sweeps and frees.

The dawn will break, yet still we stay,
In tender warmth, we drift and sway.
With every murmur, every sigh,
Our souls converse, as time slips by.

Forever held in love's embrace,
In every heartbeat, there's your grace.
Through whispered words and autumn's chill,
Murmurs soft, my heart you fill.

Timeless Resonance

Across the ages, echoes sway,
As time unfolds in shades of gray.
A resonance that breaks the dawn,
In every note, our hearts are drawn.

In quiet moments, we align,
Your spirit dances, so divine.
With every breath, a timeless song,
In harmony, we both belong.

The winds of change, they softly blow,
Yet in this love, we surely grow.
With every heartbeat, worlds collide,
In you, my love, I will confide.

The stars above, they shine so bright,
Reflecting dreams, igniting light.
In every glance, a story weaves,
Through boundless skies, our heart believes.

Together lost, we forge our fate,
In timeless dance, we celebrate.
As echoes fade, we still remain,
In love's sweet song, we shall sustain.

Shadows of Sweet Surrender

In twilight's glow, our spirits meet,
With every heartbeat, love's retreat.
Shadows loom, yet fear takes flight,
In sweet surrender, we find light.

With open arms, we face the dusk,
In trust and faith, love's gentle husk.
Through whispered dreams, we drift away,
In dusky hues, we choose to stay.

The world dissolves, as we embrace,
Within the dark, we find our place.
With every kiss, the night unfolds,
Our secrets kept, like treasures gold.

As moonlight bathes our souls in peace,
In shadows' dance, our worries cease.
With every sigh, the heart surrenders,
In timeless hours, love's sweet splendor.

Together lost, beneath the stars,
In shadowed whispers, love's memoirs.
With joyful hearts, we softly tender,
The shadows of our sweet surrender.

Distant Songs of Passion

From distant shores, the echoes rise,
Like whispers carried through the skies.
A melody that stirs the soul,
In every note, we find our whole.

The drums of love, they beat so strong,
As distant voices sing our song.
In twilight's glow, our passions flare,
A fiery warmth, beyond compare.

With every glance, we chase the night,
In dreams adorned with purest light.
Across the hills, the music flows,
In every heartbeat, love bestows.

Through distant lands, our spirits soar,
With each sweet song, we long for more.
In passion's grip, we lose control,
Dancing to rhythms of the whole.

The world fades out; it's just us two,
In distant songs, forever true.
With every breath, the night ignites,
In symphonies of endless heights.

The Tangle of Hearts

In the garden where dreams intertwine,
Two souls dance, a rhythm divine.
Whispers of love in the twilight air,
A tapestry woven, fragile and rare.

Through shadows cast, they find a way,
Beneath the stars where hopes sway.
Moments stitched with threads of gold,
In every glance, a story told.

Bound by fate, yet free to roam,
In tangled vines, they make their home.
With every pull, their passions ignite,
A love that blooms in the still of night.

Yet storms may come, with thunder loud,
Testing the roots where dreams are proud.
But through the rain, their bond will stay,
A promise held, come what may.

In the quiet, they pause to reflect,
On the path they've forged, a deep connect.
With hands entwined, they face the dawn,
In the tangle of hearts, they carry on.

Embracing the Afterglow

When the day gives way to night,
Soft embers glow, a gentle light.
In the hush where silence reigns,
Love's warmth lingers, in sweet refrains.

The colors fade, yet hearts ignite,
In the afterglow, everything feels right.
Moments cherished, softly held dear,
A melody played, for only us to hear.

As shadows dance with the fading sun,
Together we'll bask, our journey begun.
Through whispered dreams and soft caress,
In this twilight, we find our rest.

Let worries drift with the passing breeze,
In this sanctuary, our souls find ease.
Boundless hopes woven in twilight hue,
Embracing the afterglow, just us two.

As time unspools, we linger and sway,
In the embrace of dusk's tender play.
With every heartbeat, we let love flow,
Wrapped in the magic of afterglow.

Shades of Us

In a world painted with myriad hues,
We find our path, our own muse.
Dancing through life, hand in hand,
Creating memories, beautifully planned.

From laughter bright to sadness profound,
In every shade, our love is found.
Through storms we stand, through sunshine we thrive,
In the palette of life, together we strive.

The canvas shifts with each passing day,
In vibrant strokes, come what may.
With every encounter, our colors blend,
In shades of us, love knows no end.

In quiet moments, our spirits ignite,
Painting dreams under starlit night.
Every glance, a brushstroke fair,
In shades of us, we lay our hearts bare.

So let the world with its colors collide,
In this masterpiece, forever abide.
With every heartbeat, our stories entwine,
In the shades of us, our hearts align.

Unfolding the Past

In the silence, secrets lie still,
Echoes of time, a haunting thrill.
With every breath, we trace the line,
Unfolding the past, in shadows we shine.

Old photographs tell stories we know,
Whispers of moments that shaped our glow.
Each wrinkle of time, a tale to see,
In the folds of memory, you and me.

The laughter shared and the tears we cried,
In the journey of life, we never hide.
Each chapter written, love's guiding light,
Unfolding the past, making it right.

With open hearts, we face what was,
Embracing the beauty of every cause.
In the tapestry woven, every strand,
Unfolding the past, together we stand.

As we move forward, hand in hand,
The whispers of yesteryear softly expand.
In the heart's garden, where memories cast,
Together we thrive, unfolding the past.

The Tides of Belonging

In the waves we find our way,
Together we dance, come what may,
Soft whispers call from the shore,
In every tide, we ask for more.

Hands intertwined, hearts open wide,
A journey shared, a gentle ride,
With every rise, we grow more strong,
In the embrace where we belong.

Moments drift like grains of sand,
Forging bonds we understand,
The ocean's song sings sweet and clear,
Reminding us, we are always near.

Beneath the sun, under the moon,
Together we'll hum our own tune,
As the tides wash away the doubt,
In this love, there's never a drought.

Through every storm, our roots grow deep,
In the promise of love, we'll keep,
With every wave, a chance to claim,
The beauty found in our shared name.

Tapestries of Togetherness

Threads of laughter, woven tight,
Colors blend in morning light,
Each moment stitched, a tale to tell,
In this fabric, we find our spell.

Patterns dance in joyous flow,
Every loop, a chance to grow,
Shared secrets and dreams we weave,
In this quilt of love, we believe.

Hands create with steady grace,
Finding warmth in every space,
Heartfelt stitches, bold and bright,
We craft our world in pure delight.

With every turn, new stories rise,
A tapestry beneath the skies,
In tangled threads, we find our way,
Celebrating every single day.

Together we stand, stitching life,
Binding joy, lifting strife,
In every fiber, our spirits soar,
In this tapestry, forevermore.

Mosaic of Moments

Bits of laughter, shards of cheer,
Fragments held so very dear,
Each piece shines, uniquely bright,
Creating beauty in the light.

Colors clash, then harmonize,
Painting memories that arise,
In the canvas of our hearts,
Art unfolds as life imparts.

Tiny whispers, mounting dreams,
In the quiet, hope redeems,
Together we shape our design,
In this mosaic, your hand in mine.

Every crack tells a story true,
Reflecting all we've been through,
With each moment, we build anew,
A masterpiece that is just us two.

Life's a puzzle, piece by piece,
In shared moments, we find our peace,
Bonding through the joy we've sown,
In this mosaic, we are home.

The Soundtrack of You and I

In notes that drift through the air,
Melodies whisper, soft and rare,
Each heartbeat plays a subtle tone,
In this rhythm, we are not alone.

The chorus rises, strong and sweet,
Harmony found in every beat,
With laughter woven in the song,
We create a world where we belong.

Moments echo, pure and clear,
Every silence holds you near,
Together we write our refrain,
In the music, joy remains.

Dancing through the highs and lows,
In every change, our love still grows,
The soundtrack plays, forever true,
Every note a piece of you.

As the final note fades away,
Our symphony will always stay,
In the hearts that know our song,
The soundtrack of us, where we belong.

Tides of Fondness

Waves whisper secrets to the shore,
With each ebb, I crave you more.
Moonlit dances upon the sea,
Tides echo, you belong with me.

In the quiet of the night,
Stars twinkle, oh so bright.
The ocean's heart calls our name,
Forever bound, in love's sweet game.

Gentle breezes kiss our skin,
In this moment, we begin.
Let the currents pull us near,
With each tide, I hold you dear.

As the sun begins to rise,
Golden light, a soft surprise.
Together, we embrace the dawn,
In this dance, we carry on.

The rolling waves, they softly glide,
In their rhythm, love won't hide.
Endless, like the ocean wide,
In life's tide, we will abide.

Soft Footprints in the Sand

Barefoot wanderers on the beach,
Our hearts in harmony, within reach.
Each step we take, a mark we leave,
In the sand, our dreams weave.

A gentle touch, a soft embrace,
Together, we find our place.
With every wave that comes and goes,
Our love in the air, it softly flows.

Sunset hues paint the sky,
Hand in hand, you and I.
As the shadows start to blend,
Each moment here, we transcend.

The whispers of the sea, so sweet,
Echo our hearts, a perfect beat.
In this solitude, we grow,
With each other, we let go.

As night falls, stars emerge,
In our dreams, we will surge.
Soft footprints, a tale untold,
In this journey, love unfolds.

Silhouettes of Emotion

In twilight's glow, shadows dance,
Silhouettes weave a mystic romance.
Every glance, a story told,
In the silence, our hearts unfold.

Moonlight bathes our tender forms,
Wrapped in warmth, as magic swarms.
Fleeting moments, soft and pure,
In this embrace, we find our cure.

Whispers carried on the breeze,
In your arms, time seems to freeze.
Here we stand, two souls entwined,
In the night, love is defined.

As dawn approaches, we hold tight,
To silhouettes fading with light.
Memories etched against the glow,
In our hearts, forever flow.

In every shadow, love remains,
Through light and dark, through joys and pains.
Together, we face every storm,
In silhouettes, our spirits warm.

Dreamscapes of Us

In twilight dreams, we softly soar,
Past the clouds, forevermore.
Hand in hand, we chase the stars,
In dreamscapes, we journey far.

Whispers of love fill the air,
With every heartbeat, we declare.
In the quiet of our night,
Our souls embrace in soft moonlight.

Painted skies full of delight,
With you, every moment's bright.
We sketch our dreams upon the skies,
In this space, true magic lies.

Through the valleys of our mind,
In every corner, love we find.
With each breath, a wish anew,
In this dream, it's me and you.

As dawn approaches, dreams may wane,
But in our hearts, they will remain.
Dreamscapes of us, a timeless tale,
In love's embrace, we will not fail.

The Reverse Silhouette

In twilight's gentle sway, shadows dance,
Echoes of day, in a fleeting glance.
Beneath the moon, secrets take flight,
A canvas of dreams, painted in night.

Figures once bold, now fade away,
Whispers of light, in shades of gray.
What was once clear, now lost to time,
Revealing a tale, so bittersweet, sublime.

Every outline speaks, of stories untold,
Fleeting impressions, in the night cold.
Silhouettes linger, in silence they stay,
Holding the past, as night turns to day.

A breath of the night, hangs heavy with sighs,
Each shadow a truth, under starlit skies.
In the reverse, we find what's real,
The heart of the matter, the scars, the heal.

Here in this haven, all fears set free,
A journey of self, in the mystery.
Embraced by the dark, we learn to forgive,
In the silhouette's arms, our spirits may live.

Violin of Vulnerability

In the hush of night, a string softly weeps,
Notes of the heart, in every heartache leaps.
Emotions laid bare, like a canvas of sound,
In vulnerability's embrace, solace is found.

Each bow's gentle stroke, a whispering plea,
Crafted with care, a raw symphony.
Fraying at edges, yet tender and true,
In every sharp note, love breaks through.

Wounds of the past, painted in notes,
Echoing softly, where silence floats.
A dance of despair, with grace intertwined,
The violin speaks, where words fall behind.

Resonance lingers, in the depths we find,
Beauty in sorrow, uniquely designed.
With each trembling chord, our stories unfold,
In the realm of the heart, where the brave and bold.

As the final refrain, fades gently away,
We embrace the truth, in the music we play.
Violin of vulnerability, a haunting embrace,
Reminding us all, of love's fragile grace.

Flames of Forgotten Passion

In the hearth of the heart, embers still glow,
Whispers of love, from long ago.
Flickers of warmth, in the cold night air,
Memories linger, both fragile and rare.

The fire once raged, danced with delight,
Now smoldering softly, a dim flickering light.
Ashes of laughter and tears left to weep,
In the silence that follows, old promises sleep.

Winds of change blow, through the quiet room,
Yet the spark of the past, still fights against gloom.
In the depth of the night, sparks twist and bend,
Rekindling the joy, that love can transcend.

Once vibrant and bright, now shadows remain,
A tapestry woven with loss and with gain.
Catch the last breath, before it departs,
Flames of forgotten, still warm in our hearts.

As we raise our voices, to the flickers so shy,
We hold on to dreams that refuse to die.
In the dance of the embers, our souls intertwine,
Flames of forgotten passion, forever divine.

The Glow of Shared Moments

In the hush of the dawn, we linger in light,
Moments like stars, piercing the night.
With laughter we weave, a tapestry bright,
In the glow of together, everything feels right.

Each smile a beacon, guiding us home,
Creating a warmth, through the paths that we roam.
In silence we speak, with glances so clear,
The glow of shared moments, forever held dear.

Like flickering candles, illuminating truth,
We cherish the days, the spark of our youth.
With hands intertwined, and hearts open wide,
In the glow of connection, love cannot hide.

With every embrace, time seems to fold,
Collecting our stories, both timid and bold.
In the canvas of life, we paint with delight,
The glow of shared moments, our guiding light.

As sunsets fade softly, we gather the threads,
Underneath twilight, where fondness spreads.
In laughter and warmth, we know we belong,
The glow of shared moments, our second skin song.

Sensing the Unsaid

In whispers soft, the secrets lie,
Words unspoken, ready to fly.
Silent gazes, knowing glance,
In the quiet, we find our dance.

Emotions tangled, hearts entwined,
In the stillness, truths unlined.
A touch can speak what lips won't say,
In shadows cast, we find our way.

The air is thick with all that's felt,
In hidden corners, feelings dwelt.
Unraveling threads of the unheard,
In the silence, a symphony stirred.

Echoes linger, soft and light,
Shadows revel in pure delight.
Each heartbeat beats an ancient tune,
In the twilight, we find our moon.

Beyond the words, a world awaits,
In muted dreams, love creates.
With every sigh, a story told,
In the unsaid, our hearts unfold.

Resonant Dreams

In the silence, dreams take flight,
Painting colors in the night.
Whispers echo, life's sweet theme,
In every heartbeat, a resonant dream.

Stars above, a guiding hand,
In this world, we understand.
Chasing shadows, light's embrace,
In twilight's glow, we find our place.

Together we dance, souls aligned,
In the fabric of time, intertwined.
Hopes like fireflies, brightly gleam,
In the dance of a vibrant dream.

Through the silence, visions weave,
In the quiet, we believe.
Moments linger, soft and warm,
In every dream, a hidden charm.

Awake or sleeping, joy remains,
Resonating through our veins.
In the whispers of the night,
We chase our dreams, we find our light.

Enchanted by Recollections

Fleeting moments, softly caught,
In memories, all we sought.
Time unfolds in gentle grace,
In every smile, a warm embrace.

Echoes linger through the years,
In the laughter, in the tears.
Treasured tales that softly gleam,
In our hearts, they softly beam.

Woven threads of joy and pain,
In the sun and in the rain.
Every glance, a journey shared,
In every moment, true love bared.

Paths once crossed, now memories bright,
Guiding us through darkest night.
With every whisper, a trace of light,
In recollections, we take flight.

Spirits dance in twilight's glow,
In the stillness, love will flow.
Enchanted by those times we knew,
In remembrance, we find what's true.

The Flicker of Fleeting Moments

Each second slips like grains of sand,
In our grasp, we understand.
The flicker shines, a fleeting spark,
In laughter's echoes, we leave a mark.

Days roll on, a rushing stream,
In every heartbeat, a transient dream.
Moments precious, caught in flight,
In the twilight, soft and bright.

Time a thief, yet a gentle friend,
In its grasp, we weave and mend.
In stolen glances, we find delight,
In fleeting moments, we take flight.

Whispered secrets on the breeze,
Memories float like autumn leaves.
Caught in time's embrace, we roam,
In every flicker, we find home.

So hold me close, as shadows blend,
In fleeting moments, love transcend.
For life's a dance, swift and free,
In every heartbeat, you and me.

Memories that Embrace

In the quiet dusk of twilight's glow,
We gather the whispers from long ago.
Fragments of laughter, shadows that play,
In the heart's deep chamber, they softly stay.

Each moment a treasure, wrapped in delight,
The warmth of remembering holds us tight.
Through laughter and tears, we find our way,
In the memories that never decay.

Glimmers of joy in the rearview's cast,
Time may move on, but the feelings last.
With every heartbeat, we hold them near,
In a dance of remembrance, crystal clear.

Like petals unfolding in radiant light,
Each memory blooms, so precious, so bright.
A tapestry woven with golden thread,
Stories we share, the things left unsaid.

In the silence, we find solace and peace,
The love in our memories will never cease.
Embracing the echoes, both old and new,
In the garden of time, we always renew.

The Lullaby of Our Souls

Softly the night whispers secrets so sweet,
As stars above dance to a rhythmic beat.
A lullaby drifts on a gentle breeze,
Wrapping our hearts with harmonious ease.

The moonlight, a guardian, watches us dream,
In the quiet, our spirits together seem.
With every breath, a song fills the air,
A melody woven with love and care.

Close your eyes now, let worries unfold,
In the warmth of this night, be brave and be bold.
For here in the silence, our souls intertwine,
In a symphony crafted by fate's design.

We'll sway to the music of starlit skies,
As the universe hums lullabies,
With echoes of dreams that never grow old,
In the embrace of our love, we are consoled.

Each note a reminder of moments we share,
In the hush of the night, there's beauty laid bare.
A lullaby cradles both tender and true,
As we weave our dreams in cottony blue.

Cadence of Togetherness

In the rhythm of life, we find our song,
Two hearts united, where we belong.
With every heartbeat, we dance to the flow,
In this cadence of love, our spirits aglow.

Through trials and triumphs, hand in hand,
We navigate life, together we stand.
In the laughter that echoes, in tears that may fall,
This harmony binds us, our love is the call.

Step by step, as the seasons may change,
Through moments of joy, through pathways and strange.
With a grace that endures, we journey as one,
In the cadence of togetherness, we've just begun.

Through silence and words, in whispers so clear,
The rhythm of hearts beats steady and near.
In every embrace, a story unfolds,
In the dance of our lives, together we're bold.

The melody that lingers, soft and divine,
In the tapestry of days, our fates intertwine.
In this beautiful dance, we'll forever stay,
In the cadence of togetherness, come what may.

Unrealized Dreams

In the shadows of night, dreams start to fade,
Wishes unspoken, in silence they wade.
Chasing the visions we let slip away,
In the corners of hope, where memories play.

With every heartbeat, a desire ignites,
A flicker of passion that longs for the lights.
But time can deceive and the years can mislead,
Leaving behind all the things that we need.

Like flowers in winter, they yearn for the sun,
Unrealized dreams, still hoping to run.
In the garden of thought, they silently grow,
Waiting for moments when we dare to show.

Yet in the stillness, a spark can remain,
An echo of laughter that dances like rain.
Through the veil of regret, we'll learn to believe,
In the beauty of dreams, we still can achieve.

So let's gather courage, dress in the light,
Awaken the visions that blur in the night.
For unrealized dreams are but steps to embrace,
A journey of love, a boundless space.

Unforgotten Voices

In the echoes of time, their whispers remain,
A chorus of memories that linger through pain.
Unforgotten voices that speak from the past,
Remind us of moments that forever will last.

Each story a thread in the fabric of fate,
With lessons and laughter, we carry their weight.
In the sepia tones of the heart's old refrain,
Unforgotten voices call out in the rain.

From shadows they rise, like phantoms of light,
Illuminating paths that once felt so right.
They guide us through storms, through heartache and joy,

In the symphony played, they never destroy.

So let us remember, each name etched in time,
The voices that cherish the mountains we climb.
In the cadence of life, their wisdom imparts,
Unforgotten, they live in our very own hearts.

With every heartbeat, their love reshapes,
The echoes of laughter, the tender escapes.
For in the silence, their presence we find,
Unforgotten voices, forever entwined.

Tones of Trust

In whispers soft, our secrets share,
A bond that forms in silent care.
Through storms we stand, united strong,
In gentle hearts, where we belong.

Eyes like mirrors, reflecting true,
Each gesture speaks, our spirits grew.
In laughter light, or burdens shared,
In every moment, we have fared.

The echoes of our promises ring,
With every challenge, new songs we sing.
In every touch, in every glance,
Together, always, we advance.

In times of doubt, when shadows loom,
Our friendship's glow will pierce the gloom.
With faith as strong as iron chain,
In trust's embrace, we feel no pain.

The tapestry of life we've spun,
With threads of gold, we've just begun.
In every challenge, hope abounds,
In tones of trust, our love resounds.

Clarity in the Chaos

In swirling winds, the thoughts collide,
Yet in the storm, calm minds abide.
With every wave, confusion strains,
But through the storm, a path remains.

Among the noise, a voice rings clear,
A beacon bright, to draw us near.
In tangled webs, there lies a thread,
That weaves the peace where angels tread.

When chaos reigns and shadows creep,
In quiet moments, we must leap.
For clarity, a choice we make,
To seek the truth, for sanity's sake.

The heart responds to gentle light,
In darkest paths, it shines so bright.
With every breath, let worries fade,
In clarity, our fears are laid.

Through shifting sands, our spirits rise,
With courage found, we face the skies.
In every challenge, calm we find,
A radiant strength, forever kind.

Fluttering Notes of Nostalgia

In quiet rooms where echoes soar,
Old melodies play, we seek for more.
With every note, our hearts unwind,
In fleeting moments, joy defined.

The laughter shared in summers past,
In every whisper, shadows cast.
With every song, the memories dance,
In fluttering notes, we find our chance.

Through window panes, the world goes by,
Yet in our hearts, sweet voices sigh.
In photographs, the seasons change,
Each fleeting touch, forever strange.

Time may wear the edges thin,
But in our hearts, the songs begin.
In timeless tales, we hold them tight,
Fluttering notes, like stars in night.

Across the years, the feelings blend,
In every verse, old dreams transcend.
In notes that flutter like a sigh,
Nostalgia lives, it will not die.

The Light Beneath the Surface

Beneath the waves, a world awaits,
Where hidden truths, in silence, states.
In depths unknown, the colors burst,
A beauty veiled, yet deeply thirst.

In murky waters, shadows play,
Yet light will find its whispered way.
With every dive, the heart will seek,
The treasures there, though they seem weak.

Rippling tales from ages past,
In every glimmer, shadows cast.
Our spirits dance in vibrant streams,
In silent depths, we forge our dreams.

A gentle sun breaks through the dark,
Awakening the hidden spark.
In every shimmer, hope arrives,
The light beneath, where magic thrives.

With every stroke, we break the bound,
In currents strong, our hopes resound.
Through depths unknown, our journey flows,
The light beneath, forever glows.

Ripples of Connection

In the stillness of the lake,
Ripples dance with gentle grace.
Each moment shared between us,
Leaves an echo in this space.

A glance exchanged, a soft smile,
Threads of warmth begin to weave.
In this tapestry of life,
We find beauty in belief.

Hands entwined, heartbeats grow,
Each touch ignites the fire.
With every laugh, love's river flows,
Carrying dreams, our greatest desires.

Like the moon that pulls the tide,
Your presence draws me near.
In your eyes, I see the stars,
Guiding us without fear.

Together we create a path,
In the vastness of the night.
As the ripples fade away,
Our souls shine ever bright.

The Language of Touch

Fingers brush like a soft breeze,
Words unspoken, hearts communicate.
In each caress, a story unfolds,
A bond that time cannot placate.

Warmth flows through fingertips,
Tracing lines of memories shared.
In your embrace, I find solace,
A world where love is declared.

Every heartbeat resonates deep,
Each gesture speaks of our truth.
An unbroken thread of trust,
Binding the old with the youth.

As shadows lengthen and fade,
We create our own sanctuary.
In the quiet of our stillness,
Touch reveals the ordinary.

Together we dance through the unknown,
In a rhythm that feels divine.
With every stroke, we write our tale,
In the language that is purely thine.

Memories in the Wind

Whispers carried on the breeze,
Echoes of laughter, scents of the past.
Time spins threads of golden memories,
Moments we wish could forever last.

The rustling leaves call your name,
A symphony of days gone by.
Every gust, a fleeting remnant,
That dances under the vast sky.

In the air, stories take flight,
Tales of love and dreams we spun.
Together through summers and storms,
A tapestry of us well done.

As the sun sets, colors combine,
Painting memories in hues so bright.
In the twilight, we find solace,
Wrapped in the whispers of the night.

With each breeze that brushes past,
I hold those moments close and tight.
For in the wind, we are timeless,
Bound forever in this flight.

A Symphony of Us

In the garden where we bloom,
A melody begins to rise.
Notes of laughter, harmony's tune,
Composed beneath the vast skies.

Together, we create a sound,
A symphony rich and deep.
With every heartbeat, love resounds,
In the silence, secrets keep.

In the rhythm of our days,
Each moment dances with flair.
Like the music that sways,
We find solace in the air.

Your voice, a gentle serenade,
Plays the strings of my soul's core.
In this concert we have made,
I crave, I cherish, I explore.

As the final notes fade away,
Let the echoes linger still.
In the melody of our play,
I find my heart, forever filled.

Ballad of What Once Was

In the whispers of the night,
Memories linger, soft and light.
Echoes of laughter, shadows play,
Faded dreams just slip away.

Once we danced beneath the stars,
Counting wishes on our scars.
Time has woven threads so fine,
Yet in my heart, you're still mine.

Seasons change and rivers flow,
Yet the heart knows what it knows.
In silent moments, you reside,
In every tear that I have cried.

Old photographs in corners stored,
Tales of love that we adored.
Time may steal what we once shared,
But in my soul, I know you cared.

Together then, forever lost,
We bear the grief, we know the cost.
Yet in each heartbeat, you'll remain,
A bittersweet, eternal pain.

The Euphony of Emotions

Each feeling dances, a gentle breeze,
Awakening passions, bringing ease.
Joy and sorrow, intertwined,
In the heart's core, they are aligned.

Laughter bubbles, bright and free,
While tears whisper, 'Home to me.'
Melodies in twilight glow,
Each moment, a fleeting show.

Love's embrace, a tender song,
In its comfort, we belong.
Harmony in chaos found,
As life's rhythm spins around.

Dreams that linger, softly hum,
Beneath the surface, they will come.
An orchestra within the mind,
The music of the heart so kind.

So let the symphony be played,
With every note, the fears allayed.
In the euphony of feelings true,
Resides the essence crafted new.

Rhythms of the Past

Time like water flows away,
Yet memories are here to stay.
Each heartbeat whispers tales of yore,
Rhythms of life we can't ignore.

Footsteps echo down the lane,
Every joy and every pain.
In the dance of days long gone,
The past survives, it lingers on.

Faded photographs in frames,
Capture love, yet not the names.
In those moments, time stood still,
Crafting dreams against our will.

Seasons turned, the world moved on,
But in our hearts, the past lives on.
Chasing shadows, we reminisce,
In every memory, a hidden bliss.

So let us treasure what was shared,
In every smile, we once declared.
Rhythms of the past, sweet refrain,
In the silence, we feel the pain.

Chasing Faded Reminiscences

In twilight's glow, the shadows creep,
Awakening thoughts from slumber deep.
Faded memories, soft and light,
Drift like whispers in the night.

I chase the echoes, find the trace,
Of moments lost, a sweet embrace.
In the silence, voices call,
Reminiscences, they rise and fall.

With every step on paths once trod,
I feel the weight, the silent nod.
In dreams, your laughter meets my gaze,
Fleeting glimpses through the haze.

Time may blur the lines we drew,
Yet in my heart, I still see you.
Through faded pages, I will roam,
Chasing shadows, seeking home.

So let the past be my compass bright,
Guiding me through the starry night.
In every fragment, hope and joy,
Chasing dreams that love would not destroy.

Milton Keynes UK
Ingram Content Group UK Ltd.
UKHW021210291024
450281UK00021B/99

9 789916 892174